Kid's Box

Updated Second Edition

Pupil's Book 4

British English

Caroline Nixon & Michael Tomlinson

Language summary

	Key vocabulary	Key grammar and functions	Phonics
Hello there! page 4	Character names Personal descriptions **Jobs:** farmer, dentist, detective, driver, doctor, teacher	Comparative adjectives Present simple **Frequency adverbs:** always, sometimes, never have to like / love + -ing want to be	short vowel sound 'a' (m<u>a</u>n) and long vowel sounds 'ai' and 'ar' (s<u>ay</u> and c<u>ar</u>)
1 Back to school page 10	**Adjectives:** boring, busy, careful, difficult, easy, exciting, quick, slow, terrible	Relative clauses with who	short vowel sound 'i' (qu<u>i</u>ck) and long vowel sounds 'ee' and 'ie' (<u>ea</u>sy and fl<u>y</u>)
Maths Measuring page 16			
2 Good sports page 18	inside, outside **Activities:** climb, dance, fish, ride, run, sail, sing, skate, skip, swim **Adverbs of manner:** badly, carefully, easily, happily, quickly, quietly, slowly, well	Relative clauses with where learn to do (something) Adverbs of manner	silent consonants (<u>i</u>sland)
Sport Ball games page 24		Review  page 26	
3 Health matters page 28	**Health:** dentist, have a dream, have an eye test, hospital, ill, nurse, see the doctor, take some medicine	Past simple irregular verbs: affirmative, negative, interrogative and short answers Clauses with because	Consonant sounds 'b', 'f' and 'v' (<u>b</u>all, <u>ph</u>one and <u>v</u>illage)
Music Body percussion page 34			
4 After school club page 36	**Activities:** do a musical, play chess / table tennis **Ordinal numbers:** first–twentieth	Past simple regular verbs: affirmative, negative, interrogative and short answers Spelling of -ed endings	-ed endings 'd', 'id' and 't' (call<u>ed</u>, want<u>ed</u>, kick<u>ed</u>)
English literature Poems, plays and novels page 42		Review  and page 44	

	Key vocabulary	Key grammar and functions	Phonics
5 Exploring our world — page 46	**Exploring:** Antarctica, continents, exhibition, expedition, explorer, ice, make a camp, museum, school trip, ship	Past simple irregular verbs could / couldn't: ability and short answers Clauses with so Comparative of two- and three-syllable adjectives Comparative adverbs Possessive pronouns	long vowel sound 'er' (n<u>ur</u>se)
Science — Endangered animals — page 52			
6 Technology — page 54	**Technology:** button, computer, DVD, email, the internet, mobile phone, mouse, MP3 player, screen, text message, turn on, video	Past simple irregular verbs	long vowel sound 'or' (d<u>au</u>ghter)
Technology — Robots — page 60		Review 5 and 6 — page 62	
7 At the zoo — page 64	**Animals:** bat, bear, bird, blue whale, crocodile, dolphin, elephant, giraffe, kangaroo, lion, lizard, monkey, panda, parrot, polar bear, rabbit, shark, snake, tiger	Superlative of two- and three-syllable adjectives Past simple irregular verbs **Prepositions:** behind, between, in, in front of, into, next to, on, opposite, out of, under, round	the short vowel sound 'oo' and the long vowel sound 'oo' (l<u>oo</u>k and t<u>oo</u>th)
Science — Skeletons — page 70			
8 Let's party! — page 72	**Containers:** bag, bowl, bottle, box, cup, glass **Food:** cheese, pasta, sandwich, salad, soup, vegetables	**Expressions of quantity:** a cup / bag / bowl / glass / bottle / box of **Superlative adverbs:** the most quickly want someone to do (something)	one-, two- and three-syllable words
Science — Food — page 78		Review 7 and 8 — page 80	

Values 1 & 2 Value others page 82   Values 5 & 6 Be safe page 84
Values 3 & 4 Be kind page 83   Values 7 & 8 Recycle page 85
Grammar reference page 86

Hello there!

1 Look, think and answer.

1. What does Stella want to be?
2. Who's a farmer?
3. What's Simon reading?
4. Who's riding Suzy's bike?

2 Listen and check.

3 Listen again. Choose the right words.

1. Stella's **twelve** / **twenty** / **ten**. *(Stella's ten.)*
2. Simon's older than **Suzy** / **Stella** / **May**.
3. Fred is Simon's **father** / **brother** / **uncle**.
4. Simon wants to be a **farmer** / **detective** / **dentist**.
5. Grandpa Star's **funny** / **young** / **sad**.
6. Aunt May's **younger** / **older** / **smaller** than Suzy.

LOOK

Stella's **older than** Simon.
Simon's **younger than** Stella.

4 Read and match.   1 – h

 a  b  c  d  e

 f  g  h  i

1 His hair is white and curly. He's funny.
2 He's got short black hair and he's wearing sunglasses. He's hungry.
3 She's got straight grey hair. She's thirsty.
4 She's got short brown hair and she's young. She's little, but loud.
5 She's got very long blonde hair and she's beautiful. She's quiet.
6 He's got short straight red hair. He's happy.
7 She's got straight blonde hair and she wears glasses. She's clever.
8 He's got curly red hair, a beard and a moustache. He smiles a lot.
9 She's got straight black hair. She's tired.

5 Listen and say the name.

1 Who smiles a lot?   Uncle Fred.

6 Play the game.

Has he got red hair?   Is he younger than Stella?   Is he Uncle Fred?

Yes, he has.   No, he isn't.   Yes, he is.

7 Read and answer.

1 Where does Aunt May work?
2 What does she like doing?
3 Where does Uncle Fred live?
4 What time does he get up?

Aunt May's a doctor. She works in a big hospital in the city. She sometimes works during the day and she sometimes has to work at night. She doesn't like working at the weekend. She likes listening to music and taking photos.

Uncle Fred's a farmer. He lives on a farm in the country. He's got twenty-seven cows and forty-three sheep. He always gets up at five o'clock. Uncle Fred has to work in the morning, the afternoon and the evening. He sometimes works at night too. He loves working on his farm, and driving his lorry!

8 Correct the sentences. *Aunt May's a doctor.*

1 Aunt May's a bus driver.
2 She works in a big school.
3 She never works at night.
4 She likes working at the weekend.
5 Uncle Fred lives in a flat in the city.
6 He's got forty-three cows.
7 He never gets up at five o'clock.
8 He always works at night.

 **LOOK**

She **always** wears a white coat at work.
He **sometimes** works at night.
He **never** gets up at ten o'clock.

9 Look at the song and order the pictures. Listen and check.

1 – b

The morning rap,
We do it every day.
The same routine,
Now listen and say.

It's seven o'clock,
Wake up, wake up!
You must get up
And have a wash.

Come on, come on,
It's time to go.
Get dressed, get dressed!
Put on your clothes.

Run to the kitchen,
Sit on a chair.
Eat your breakfast,
Comb your hair.

The morning rap …

It's seven o'clock …

Clean your teeth.
No time to lose.
Get your bag,
Put on your shoes.

Goodbye to Mum,
Goodbye to Dad.
My friends are at school,
So I'm not sad.

The morning rap.
The morning rap.

10 Sing the song.

11 Write about your day.

I wake up at seven o'clock.
I get dressed after I get up …

7

12 Stella's phonics

A c**a**t in a b**a**g.

A sn**a**ke and a sn**ai**l in the r**ai**n.

A f**ar**mer in his c**ar**.

The f**ar**mer's parking the c**ar** in the c**ar** p**ar**k.

13 Make questions. Ask and answer.

- have / got / younger cousin
- like / snails
- can / play basketball
- catch / bus / school
- can / swim
- have / got / older brother
- wake up / eight o'clock
- have / got a pet
- want to be / doctor

Have you got a younger cousin? — Yes, I have.

Do you like snails? — No, I don't.

Can you play basketball? — Yes, I can.

1 Back to school

1 Look, think and answer.
1. Where are the children?
2. Which class are Alex and Simon in?
3. Who likes Maths?
4. What's Meera doing?

Simon Alex
Art

Stella Lenny
Maths

Meera
Sport

boring   busy   careful   difficult   easy   exciting   quick   slow   terrible

2 Listen and check.

3 Listen and match.

1 Be careful with those glasses, Sally! I am being careful! —  e

 a
 b
 c
 d
 e

 f
 g
 h
 i

4 Read and correct the text.

My teacher.
This is Mr Newton. He's my Maths teacher. He works in a school in a big city. He's very sbyu because he's got a lot of work. There are 28 children in my class. His lessons aren't wols or grinbo, they're very ecgitxin. We like his lessons because they're not ftlaudfii. It's yase to learn lots of new things with him.
Mr Newton's very fclareu when he writes, but I'm not!

5 Write about one of your teachers.

6 Read and say their names.

 Daisy    Fred    Mary    Johnny    Paul

1 This child likes being busy with lots of homework.   *Johnny*
   His hair is straight and black and he's got glasses.
2 This child loves Art and is careful at painting.
   He's got short, brown curly hair.
3 The child with straight blonde hair is very brave.
   She loves reading to her class!
4 This child with glasses thinks Maths is exciting.
   Her hair is black and curly.
5 This child with short curly blonde hair thinks Music's difficult.

7 Make sentences for your friend. Say and answer 'true' or 'false'.

The child with glasses thinks Maths is boring.   False.

8 Look, think and answer.
1 Where are the Star family?
2 Who's Mrs Star talking to?
3 Who's the Art teacher?
4 Who's the Music teacher?

9 Listen and check.

10 Play the game.

He's the teacher who's talking to Mrs Star.

Mr Newton.

LOOK

She's the woman **who's** wearing the long green skirt.
He's the man **who's** carrying the lorry.

11 Read and find.
1. They're the boys who are laughing. d
2. She's the girl who's drinking orange juice.
3. He's the boy who's wearing a red sweater.
4. They're the girls who are wearing pink dresses.
5. She's the girl who's skipping.
6. He's the boy who's throwing a ball.

12 Choose a child. Ask and answer.

Is it the boy who's reading a comic?   No, it isn't.

13 Read and say the letter. Listen and check.   1 – a

The classroom's where you learn,
The classroom's where we teach,
Lots of exciting things,
To do in our school week …

1 I teach Sport,
It's quick, not slow,
Run, jump and skip,
Go, go, go!

2 I teach English,
All I need,
Are lots of words,
And books to read.

3 I teach Maths,
It's easy to add,
But if it's wrong,
Don't be sad.

4 I teach Art,
We can paint and draw,
Careful with the paint,
Don't drop it on the floor!

The classroom's where you learn,
The classroom's where we teach,
Lots of exciting things,
To do in our school week …

14 Sing the song.

15 Stella's phonics

Six busy insects.

A smiling crocodile.

It's easy to clean a smiling crocodile's teeth.

Sixteen teeth.

16 Make questions. Ask and answer.

Do you think Maths is exciting?

No, I don't.

Maths   Art   English   difficult   exciting   easy

Find two people who …		name 1	name 2
… think Maths is exciting	Do you think Maths is exciting?		
… think Art is easy	Do you think _____?		
… think English is difficult	Do you _____?		

Maths: Measuring

Fact: The smallest house in the UK is only three metres high!

1 Read and look.

length / height

We measure length and height in metres (m), centimetres (cm) and millimetres (mm). There are ten millimetres (10 mm) in a centimetre and a hundred centimetres (100 cm) in a metre.

2 🎧 CD1 18 Listen and say the letter.

1 Sixty-four centimetres. — f

- a 17 mm
- b 38 cm
- c 39.67 m
- d 83 m
- e 75.12 m
- f 64 cm
- g 62 mm
- h 93.56 m

3 Read and choose the answer.

1 How high is it?
a 9.6 m
b 96 cm
c 96 m

2 How long is it?
a 76.3 m
b 42.8 m
c 72 mm

3 How tall is it?
a 95 cm
b 5.9 m
c 9.5 m

4 How tall is he?
a 2.31 m
b 1.8 m
c 3.9 m

LOOK

2.45 m — two metres forty-five centimetres

16

4 Measure the things in your classroom.

pencil	11 cm
desk	
Activity Book	
eraser	
me	

How long is your pencil?
How high is your desk?
How long is your Activity Book?
How long is your eraser?
How tall are you?

Project Do a class survey. Draw a graph.

How tall are you?

One metre thirty centimetres.

How many children in your group ...		
a are taller than 1.35 m?	How tall are you?	4
b have got arms which are shorter than 60 cm?	How long are your arms?	
c have got feet which are longer than 28 cm?	How long are your feet?	
d have got little fingers which are shorter than 3 cm?		
e have got hair which is longer than 10 cm?		

2 Good sports

1 Look, think and answer.
1. Who do you think wants to climb?
2. How many water sports can they do?
3. Where can they do water sports?
4. Which activity can they do inside and outside?

2 Listen and check.

3 Listen and say the letter.

"1 He's learning to skate." "h"

LOOK

What can I **learn to** do?   You can **learn to** sail and fish.
It's a place **where** you can learn to do lots of exciting sports.

4 Make five true sentences. Use the words in the boxes.

"My teacher wants to learn to climb."

I	wants to	learn to	sail.
My teacher	doesn't want to		dance.
	want to		climb.
My friends	don't want to		ice skate.
			skip.

5 Say the places.

park   ~~lake~~   swimming pool   road   sea

1 A place where you can go ice skating. "Lake."
2 A place where you mustn't roller skate.
3 A place where you can learn to swim.
4 A place where you can learn to ride a bike.
5 A place where you can learn to sail.

6 In pairs guess the place or person. You can only ask four questions.

Jim   Jack   Sally and Paul

"Is it a person?"
"Yes, it is."
"Is it the girl who's learning to swim?"
"No, it isn't."

"Is it a place?"
"Yes, it is."
"Is it the place where you mustn't roller skate?"
"It's a road."
"Yes, it is."

7 Look, think and answer.
1 Where's Mr Star?
2 Who's climbing?
3 Where is Grandpa Star?
4 What's Suzy doing?

badly   carefully   quickly   slowly   well

8 🎧 Listen and check.

9 Read and choose the right words.
1 They're running **quietly** / **quickly** / **slowly**. *Quickly.*
2 They're shouting **loudly** / **quietly** / **carefully**.
3 He's playing **badly** / **loudly** / **well**.
4 She's riding her bike **carefully** / **quietly** / **quickly**.
5 They're reading **quietly** / **loudly** / **badly**.
6 They're running **quickly** / **well** / **slowly**.
7 He's playing **well** / **loudly** / **badly**.
8 He's riding his bike **carefully** / **loudly** / **quickly**.

10 Listen and say 'yes' or 'no'.

> 1 They're playing well.

> Yes.

11 Read and say the letter. Listen and check.

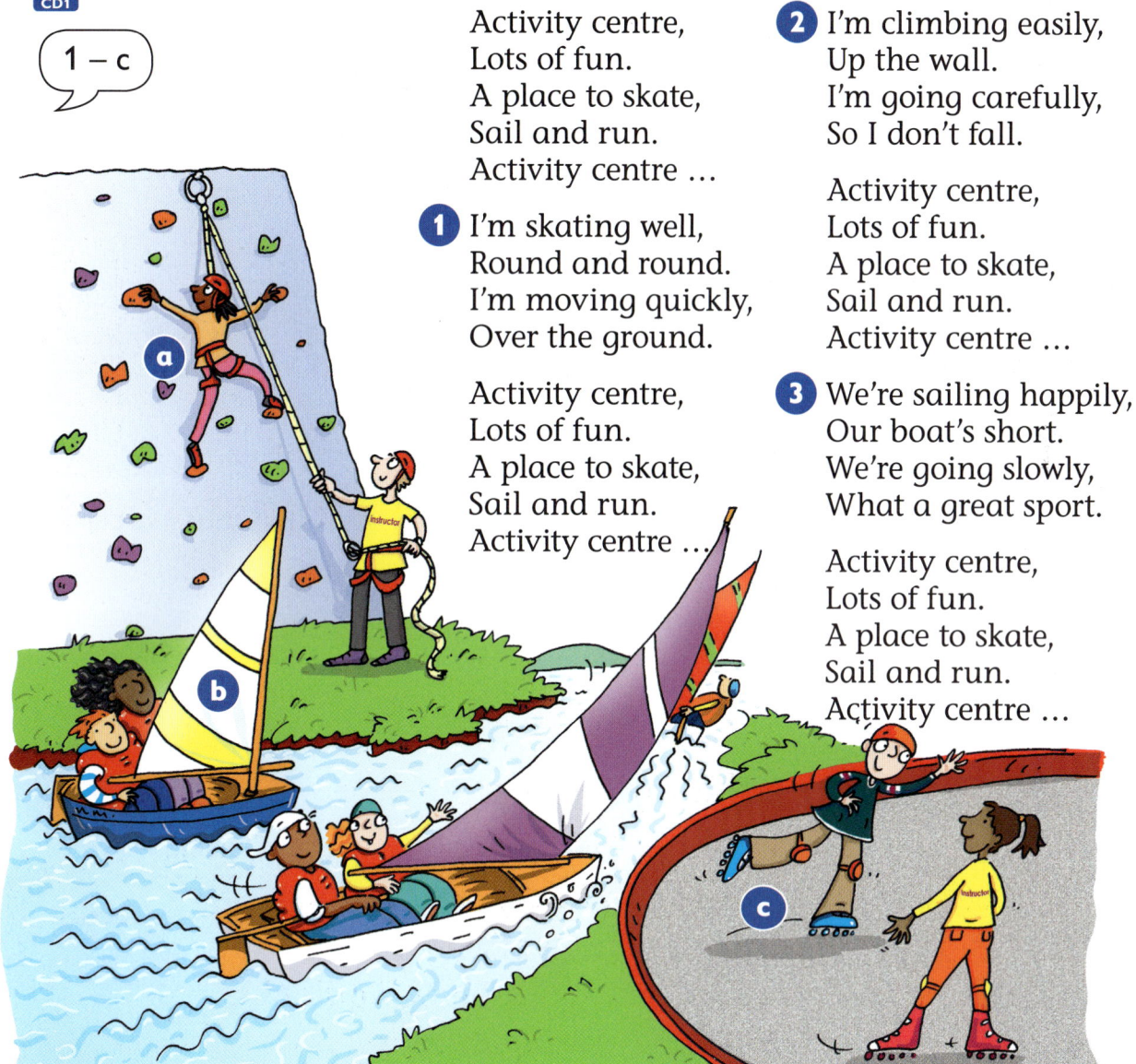

> 1 – c

Activity centre,
Lots of fun.
A place to skate,
Sail and run.
Activity centre …

1 I'm skating well,
Round and round.
I'm moving quickly,
Over the ground.

Activity centre,
Lots of fun.
A place to skate,
Sail and run.
Activity centre …

2 I'm climbing easily,
Up the wall.
I'm going carefully,
So I don't fall.

Activity centre,
Lots of fun.
A place to skate,
Sail and run.
Activity centre …

3 We're sailing happily,
Our boat's short.
We're going slowly,
What a great sport.

Activity centre,
Lots of fun.
A place to skate,
Sail and run.
Activity centre …

12 Sing the song.

13 Write another verse. Sing.

I'm **running** / **dancing** / **skipping** well,
Look at me.
Doing it **slowly** / **quickly** / **happily**,
Now you can see.

> I'm dancing well,
> Look at me.

14 Stella's phonics

A scientist is listening to music.

His daughter is eating a sandwich.

They mustn't climb on this island!

15 Ask and find your partner.

What do you want to do?
I want to go swimming and cycling.

What do you want to do?
I want to go climbing and sailing.

Sport — Ball games

1 Read and match. 1 – c

> **Fact**
> The first basketball was brown.

baseball 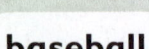   basketball

My favourite sport is baseball. You play baseball on (1)**a field** with (2)**a little white ball**, called a baseball. You hit the ball with (3)**a long bat**. There are two teams with nine players. One team throws and catches the ball. The other team hits the ball.

There are four bases: first base, second base, third base and fourth base. When a player hits the ball they run round the bases. When they arrive at fourth base they get a run. The winning team is the team with more runs at the end of the game.

My favourite sport is basketball. You play basketball with (4)**a big orange ball**. There are two teams with five players. Both teams try to get points by throwing the ball into (5)**a basket**, which is 3 metres above the floor.

You can throw, run and bounce the ball, but you can't run and carry the ball at the same time. The winning team is the team with more points after 40 minutes.

2   Listen and say 'baseball' or 'basketball'.

> 1 You play with a big ball.

> Basketball.

Do you remember? Read and answer.

Baseball
1. Where do you play baseball? — *You play baseball on a field.*
2. Do you have to play with a big orange ball?
3. How many players are there in a baseball team?
4. What do you use to hit the ball?
5. How many bases are there?
6. Which base do the players have to arrive at to get a run?

Basketball
1. How many players are there in a basketball team?
2. Can you run and carry the ball at the same time?
3. How do you get points in basketball?
4. How many minutes do you play?

 Make a ball.

You need:
- 200 grams salt or sand
- 5 balloons
- scissors

1. Cut the necks off all the balloons.
2. Put the salt or sand into the first balloon.
3. Open the second balloon and put your ball inside it. Put it over the neck of the first balloon.
4. Open the third balloon and put your ball inside it.
5. Repeat with the fourth balloon.
6. Put the last balloon over the ball. Now you're ready to play.

Review Units  1 and 2

1 Play the game.

Instructions
Red – Whose is it / are they?
Blue – What's this?
Grey – What's he / she doing?

2 Read the text and choose the best answer.

Example
Tony: Hi, Sue. What are you doing?
Sue: A I'm playing badminton.
B I'm playing baseball.
C I'm hitting the ball.

Questions

1 Tony: Who are you playing with?
Sue: A She's my Aunt Sue.
B My brother, Alex.
C We're playing well.

2 Tony: Is he older than you?
Sue: A No, he's my brother.
B Yes, he's holding the ball.
C No, he's a year younger than me.

3 Tony: Are you good at badminton?
Sue: A Yes, I've got three.
B I'm not bad, but Alex is better than me.
C No, thank you.

4 Sue: Do you like badminton?
Tony: A Yes, it's my favourite sport.
B Yes, please.
C Yes, let's.

5 Sue: Would you like to play badminton with us?
Tony: A I'd like that, thanks.
B Yes, I like board games.
C No, I prefer tennis.

6 Sue: Shall I start?
Tony: A Yes, I want to stop.
B No, I want to play.
C Yes, good idea.

Quiz!
1 Which lesson are Alex and Simon busy in?
2 Who's the teacher playing the guitar at the school show?
3 Where do Peter and his friends have their picnic?
4 What does Suzy want to learn?
5 How's Simon climbing?
6 Where do Lock and Key go on Thursday morning?

3 Health matters

1 Look, think and answer.
1 What was Simon's temperature?
2 Where was Simon on Thursday?
3 Why were Simon and his mother at the hospital?
4 When was Simon well again?

Monday   Tuesday   Wednesday   Thursday   Friday

was   were   had   drank   saw   gave   took   went   ate

2 🔊 31 CD1 Listen and check.

3 🔊 32 CD1 Listen and say the day.

1 The doctor gave him some medicine.   Wednesday.

4 Read and say the letter.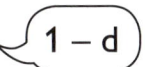

1 He took some medicine because he had a cold.

2 We ate a lot because we were hungry.

3 She went to bed early because she was sick.

4 I drank a lot because I had a temperature.

5 The doctor gave her some medicine because she had a stomach-ache.

6 They saw the dentist because they had a toothache.

5 Look and answer. Say 'Tom', 'Sue' or 'the nurse'.

   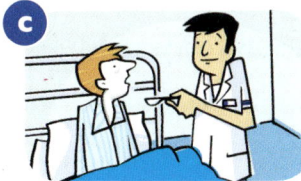 

1 Who saw the nurse? Tom.
2 Who went to the hospital to see Tom?
3 Who had a headache?
4 Who gave Tom some medicine?
5 Who ate lunch in bed?
6 Who had an eye test?
7 Who drank orange juice?
8 Who took some medicine?

6 Look, think and answer.

1 Who's Stella talking to this morning?
2 Where was Stella in her dream?
3 What was Stella's job?
4 What was wrong with the man?

7 Listen and check.

8 Answer the questions.

1 Did Stella have a nice dream?
2 Did she have a long blue coat?
3 Did she see a woman who had a cough?
4 Did she give the man some flowers?
5 Did she see a woman with backache?
6 Did she take a box off the girl's head?

🔍 **LOOK**

have → had
do → did

I **had** a terrible dream.
I **didn't have** time to stop.
How many people **did** you see?

9   Read and say the word. Listen and check.

> lemonade   ice cream   burgers   chocolate
> three   water   party   sausages   ~~nurse~~   fruit

nurse

Mummy, Mummy call the 👩‍⚕️!
I had a stomach-ache but now it's worse.

What's the matter?

I don't know,
But please be quick,
Don't be slow.

Did you have a 🎉 yesterday?

Yes! There was lots to eat and games to play.

Did you eat ?

Yes, I did.

Did you eat 🌭?

Yes, I did.

Did you drink 🍶?

Yes, I did.

Did you have 🍨 and 🍫 too?
I think I know what's the matter with you!
Take this medicine **3** times a day,
When you are better, go out and play!

No more chocolate cake for you my daughter.
Vegetables, 🍎🍌 and a drink of 🥛!

10   Sing the song.

11 Ask and answer questions about the song.

(Did she eat ice cream?)   (Yes, she did.)

(Did she drink orange juice?)   (No, she didn't.)

31

12 Stella's phonics

A frog with a phone.

A very small volleyball.

The frog and her friends are playing volleyball at the beach.

13 Ask and answer.

Did you have a temperature last week?

No, I didn't.

Health matters

1 **Did you have** a temperature last week?
2 _____ to hospital last year?
3 _____ milk for breakfast?
4 _____ a cough last year?
5 _____ an apple yesterday?
6 _____ to bed early last night?
7 _____ any medicine last week?
8 _____ the dentist last year?

~~have~~
go
eat
drink
take
see
have
go

14 Now write and ask questions about your friend's week.

Did you walk to school last week?

Music | Body percussion

Fact
The quickest person in the world can clap 12 times a second.

1 Listen and say the letter.

A percussion instrument is a musical instrument that makes a sound when we hit it. We can use different kinds of instruments or other things to make percussion music.

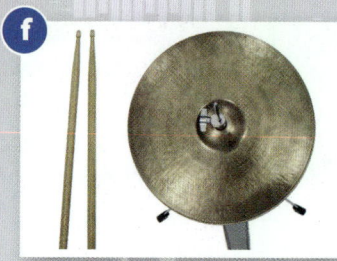

2 Listen and match. Which part of the body are they using to make the sound?

The human body is also a great percussion instrument. There are different kinds of dance and music which use parts of the body.

The language of music tells musicians what notes to play and how to play them. They can be long or short, loud or quiet, quick or slow. Rhythm tells us how long the notes are. They can be whole notes (1), half notes ($^1/_2$), quarter notes ($^1/_4$) or eighth notes ($^1/_8$). Rhythm is very important in percussion music.

3  Listen to these notes. Answer the questions.

1 Which is longer, 1 or 4?
2 Which is longer, 2 or 3?
3 Which is shorter, 1 or 2?
4 Which is shorter, 3 or 4?

4 Listen and make rhythms.

Project Make a drum.

You need:
- a plastic cup
- a balloon
- an elastic band

1 Take a piece of the balloon and put it over the top of the cup.
2 Use the elastic band to keep it in place. Now you've got a drum.

Try to make different sounds. Hit it with your hand or with a pencil. Hit it in the middle or on the edge. Try different rhythms. Play your drum to music.

4 After school club

1 Look, think and answer.

1 Where did the children go yesterday afternoon?
2 Which teacher was there?
3 Who did Stella play chess with?
4 Who wasn't good at dancing?

2 Listen and check.

3 Listen and say 'yes' or 'no'.

No.

LOOK

help	→	help**ed**
dance	→	danc**ed**
stop	→	stop**ped**
carry	→	carr**ied**

36

4 Read and match.

1 When Pat worked at a school, she was the cook. She made all the food in the morning. The children liked eating her pancakes! After lunch, Pat helped the children as they hopped, skipped and jumped in the playground.

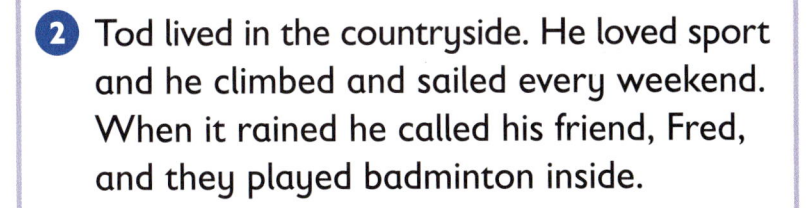

2 Tod lived in the countryside. He loved sport and he climbed and sailed every weekend. When it rained he called his friend, Fred, and they played badminton inside.

3 Yesterday David invited his friend Sid to go ice skating. It was very cold so they needed hats and scarves. It started to snow, but Sid ice skated on the lake. David pointed and shouted because Sid wasn't careful.

5 Listen and say 'a', 'b' or 'c'.

1 It started to snow. — b

6 Ask and answer.

1 Where did Pat work? — She worked at a school.
2 When did Pat cook?
3 Who loved Pat's pancakes?
4 Where did Tod live?
5 What did Tod love?
6 What did Tod and Fred play?
7 Who did David invite?
8 Why did David point and shout?

7 Look, think and answer.
1. Which friend are the children visiting?
2. Where is Alex's flat?
3. Who loves climbing?
4. Why must they walk up the stairs?

8 Listen and check.

9 Answer the questions.
1. What's the third letter of the alphabet? — c
2. What's the ninth letter?
3. What's the twelfth letter?
4. What's the sixteenth letter?
5. What's the twentieth letter?

10 Write more questions to ask your friend.

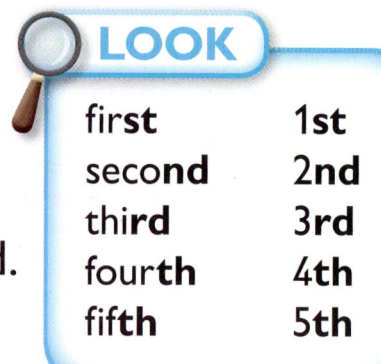

LOOK

fir**st**	1**st**
seco**nd**	2**nd**
thi**rd**	3**rd**
four**th**	4**th**
fif**th**	5**th**

11 🔊 **Listen and complete the song.**

Dancing is good, dancing is fine,
Dancing is great!
Come on, children! Dance in line!

First, second, third and fourth
Dance, dance across the floor.
_____, sixth, seventh, _____
Jump, kick, don't come in late.
_____, tenth, eleventh, _____
Dancing is _____ for your health.

Dancing's good, dancing's fine,
Come on, children! Dance in line!

Number five's _____,
And number ten's last.
He can't hop and skip,
He can't get past.

Dancing is good, dancing is fine,
Dancing is great!
Come on, children! Dance in line!

12 🔊 **Sing the song.**

13 **Ask and answer.**

Which team was first last week?

Kids United.

FOOTBALL LEAGUE TABLE
1. Kids United
2. Star Athletic
3. Heart Club
4. All Sports
5. Fit City
6. Box Runners
7. Sporting
8. Sports Kids
9. Quick Kickers
10. Dream Team
11. Great Movers
12. Cambridge Flyers
13. The Non Starters
14. Dirty Players
15. Walking Legs
16. The Hungry Sharks
17. The Goal Monsters
18. Naughty Monkeys
19. The Terrible Tigers
20. Feet First

14 Stella's phonics

Yesterday, Sam and Pam played football.

Sam got the ball and kicked it to Pam.

Oh no! They needed that goal!

15 Make questions. Ask and answer.

Did you dance to music last week?

Did you watch TV in your room last week?

Yes, I did.

No, I didn't.

walk play listen	~~to music~~ to the radio to school
help ~~watch~~ take	your mum a photo your homework
~~dance~~ do practise	table tennis ~~TV in your room~~ roller skating

Find two people who … last week		name 1	name 2
… dance to music	Did you dance to music last week?		
… watch TV in your room	Did you watch TV in your room last week?		

LOCK & KEY

Hello, Peter. What are you doing here?

I've got two tickets for my school show on Wednesday. Would you like to come?

Yes, please, Peter. Which show are you doing?

We're doing Peter Pan. Pupils and parents are in it.

We're over there in the fifth row. These are our chairs. Can you go and get us some drinks, Key?

No problem, Lock! Two lemonades.

This is great!

Look at him, Key! It's Nick Motors!

I crossed the sea and sailed to Neverland to catch you, Peter Pan!

Come down here! You, you, you ... pirate!

I know who you are! Oops!

Ow, my beard. That hurts!

Dad, this is Mr Lock. Er, Mr Lock, this is my dad.

English literature — Poems, plays and novels

1 Read and match.

a.
b.
c.

Fact
The biggest book in the world is an atlas in the British Museum. It's 1.8 m high!

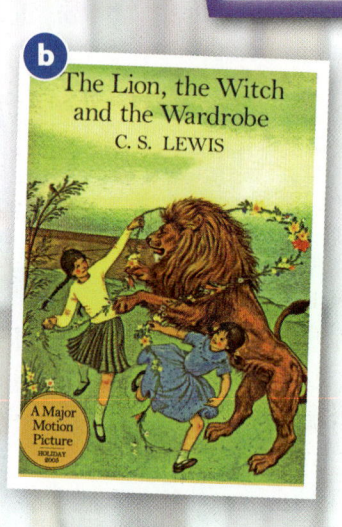

THE OWL AND THE PUSSY-CAT.

There are lots of different kinds of literature. What do you like reading?

1 Poems
The Owl and the Pussycat is a children's poem by Edward Lear.

> The Owl and the Pussycat went to sea
> In a beautiful pea-green boat,
> They took some honey, and plenty of money,
> Wrapped up in a five pound note.

2 Plays
We go to a theatre to see plays. Peter Pan by J. M. Barrie is a famous children's play about the adventures of Peter Pan, Wendy and her brothers John and Michael. They learn to fly and go to the island of Neverland, where they fight Captain Hook and his pirates.

3 Novels
C. S. Lewis is the author of The Chronicles of Narnia. There are seven books in The Chronicles of Narnia. The first is The Lion, the Witch and the Wardrobe. It is about the adventures of the Pevensie children in the country of Narnia.

2 Answer the questions.
1 What colour was the Owl and the Pussycat's boat?
2 Where does Peter Pan fight Captain Hook?
3 How many books are there in The Chronicles of Narnia?

3 Read and order the text. 1 – d

The Lion, the Witch and the Wardrobe

a One of the rooms had nothing inside it except a big old cupboard for clothes – a wardrobe. Lucy went inside and she saw a lot of coats. She walked to the back of the wardrobe.

b Lucy went back to Narnia with the other children. They helped the king, a lion, to make Narnia a happy place. Later, Peter, Susan, Edmund and Lucy were kings and queens of Narnia.

c Then there was snow on the ground and trees touched her face. Lucy was cold. She was in a forest at night.

The wardrobe was behind her. Lucy was in Narnia, where animals can talk. One of them told Lucy that a bad white witch lived in Narnia and it was always winter. All the animals were sad.

d Four children went to stay in a big house in the country. Their names were Peter, Susan, Edmund and Lucy. One day it was very rainy outside, so they played inside. It was boring, but the house had a lot of rooms to look in.

Project

Make a 'My favourite book' poster.

My favourite book
My favourite book is called ....
The author's name is ....
The story is about ....
The characters are called ....
I like it because ....

Review Units 3 and 4

1 Play the game.

Instructions

Before you play, decide which actions are good and which are bad.
Good actions: Go forward 2 spaces.
Bad actions: Go back 2 spaces.

- You helped your mum.
- You didn't do your homework.
- You went to football practice.
- You worked quickly and well.
- You talked to your friend in class.
- You were naughty in class.
- You cleaned your room.
- You were late for school because you stopped to buy a comic.
- You answered your grandpa's email.
- You carried the shopping for your grandma.

START

FINISH

2 How did Mary go to these places?
Listen and write a letter in each box. There is one example.

train — H

car —

walking —

bus —

bike —

boat —

5 Exploring our world

1 Look at Simon's homework. Think and answer.
1. Who did Simon show his homework to?
2. Who did Simon write about?
3. Who was Shackleton?
4. How did Shackleton go to Antarctica?

A famous explorer, Sir Ernest Shackleton, wanted to cross Antarctica. In 1914 he started the expedition but ice closed round the ship. They took smaller boats and made a camp on the snow. They lost their ship when it went down under the ice and water.

They couldn't move because the weather was terrible. They caught fish and drank water which they got from snow. Later, they had to eat their dogs.

Shackleton and some of his men climbed over mountains of ice, found help and went back for the other men. Everybody came home two years after the start of their expedition. They didn't cross Antarctica.

Ernest Shackleton

2 Read and check.

3 Find the past of these verbs in the text.

find   catch   take   go   make
get   can't   lose   have to   come

4 Read and say the letter. 1 – f

1 Last week David's class went to a museum.
2 First they walked round an exhibition about explorers.
3 They could read explorers' diaries, so it was really exciting.
4 Before lunch they made a poster about famous explorers.
5 After lunch they found the museum shop and David got a toy polar bear for his sister.
6 In the afternoon they went to an exhibition about sea animals.
7 Before they came home, David took a photograph of his friends.
8 At three o'clock they caught the bus home.

5 Listen and answer the questions.

1 When did David's class go to a museum?

They went to a museum last week.

6 Make sentences. They were hungry so they ate sandwiches.

1 They were hungry	they couldn't find the museum.
2 They didn't take water with them	he got a toy from the shop.
3 The exhibition was really good **so**	they ate sandwiches.
4 It was his sister's birthday	they came home late.
5 The children had to wait for the bus	they had a great time.
6 They lost their map	they were thirsty.

47

7 Look, think and answer.

1. Which explorers are Simon and Alex talking about?
2. What was Cousteau's ship called?
3. Who did Alex write about?
4. What did Cousteau explore?

Cousteau

Shackleton

8 Listen and check.

9 Complete the text.

Alex thinks that Shackleton's adventures were ___more___ difficult _____ Cousteau's, but Cousteau is _____ famous for his work. Cousteau said we have to be _____ careful with the sea. Stella thinks Simon's homework was _____ interesting _____ hers. Lenny was happy because he did his homework _____ quickly than Simon and Alex.

> **LOOK**
>
> Cousteau is **more famous** for his work.
> Our homework was **easier than** theirs.
> Shackleton sailed **more slowly than** Cousteau.

48

10 Order the words.
1. interesting / My book on explorers is / yours. / than / more
2. dangerous / more / Jacques Cousteau's. / than / Shackleton's adventures were
3. more / climbing trees. / Crossing Antarctica is / difficult / than
4. than / Jacques Cousteau. / more / Christopher Columbus is / famous
5. carefully / Suzy. / more / Simon writes / than
6. walking. / Sailing is / exciting / more / than

11 What do you think? Make sentences.

boring   exciting   dangerous   beautiful   difficult   easy

I think climbing is more dangerous than swimming.

climbing   swimming   pop music   classical music

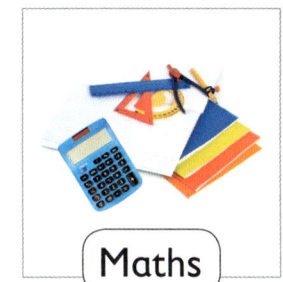

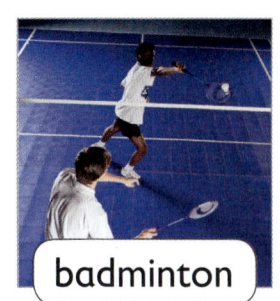

Maths   Art   badminton   table tennis

horses   fish   photo   painting

12 Now write sentences.

I think badminton is more boring than table tennis.

13 Stella's phonics

The nurse got a shirt for her birthday.

On Thursday the shirt got dirty.

The nurse worked in her purple shirt.

14 Complete the rap. Listen and check.

trees   green   ~~mine~~   ours   his   strong

The world isn't **mine**,
The world isn't yours.
The world isn't _____,
The world isn't hers.
It's ours,
It's _____!

Our world is tired, we're making mistakes,
We need our seas, we need our lakes.
Our world is weak, we can make it _____,
It needs our help. Listen to our song.

We must look after its forests and _____,
We must look after its rivers and seas.
We can make it better, we can make it _____,
This is our world, let's keep it clean.

15 Sing the song.

LOCK & KEY

Look, Key! I've got information about Nick Motors. He's on an adventure holiday in the countryside.

Good! These holidays are more exciting than holidays at the beach.

Explore Adventure Holidays

Look here. It says you can explore forests, rivers and beaches. Can we go, Lock? Please!

OK, Key. But we have to catch Nick Motors!

He came here yesterday. He caught a bus in the afternoon and had dinner in the Lakeside Restaurant.

LAKESIDE RESTAURANT

Explore Adventure Holiday Camp

We can catch him easily, Lock. No problem.

Excuse me. Do you know this man?

Oh yes! I gave him his breakfast this morning.

Hmmm, but he's not here now.

Hello! What are you doing here, Mr Key?

LAKESIDE RESTAURANT

Hello, Miss Rich. We're at work. We're trying to catch a thief.

I've got a message on my phone!

I don't understand. It says, 'Look behind you!'

He's got our bike! I need a holiday.

51

Science — Endangered animals

Fact: The name 'Arctic' comes from a Greek word meaning 'near the bear'.

1 Look. Which animals do you think are endangered?

polar bear    kangaroo    goat

Siberian tiger    panda

2 Read. Correct the sentences.

Lily wants to help the world. She wants to stop the Earth from getting hotter and the Arctic from getting smaller. She's in a society called the Green Heroes. They help endangered animals.

Polar bears live in the Arctic. They live on the ice and swim in the sea. They catch and eat other sea animals like seals, fish or small whales.
Polar bears have problems because the world is hotter than it was before. Oceans are hotter and the ice cap is smaller so polar bears are losing their habitat. Now it's more difficult for polar bears to fish for food or look after their babies if they haven't got ice to live on.

1. Polar bears live on mountains and swim in the lake.
2. They catch and eat other animals like lions, bats and pandas.
3. The world is colder than it was before.
4. It's easier for polar bears to fish for food.
5. It's more difficult for polar bears to look after their parents.

3 🎧 **Listen. Read and say 'yes' or 'no'.**
CD2 20

Listen to Lily talking to a friend about the society and their work.
1 Lily's project is called 'Help the world'.
2 The Green Heroes are young people who want to protect cars.
3 The Earth is getting colder.
4 Air in big cities is cleaner now.
5 It's a good idea to ride bikes and use public transport.
6 People are cutting down trees in forests.
7 The world needs trees to clean the air.

Project Make a poster about 'endangered animals'.

- Choose three endangered animals.
  You can use whale, dolphin, panda, penguin, polar bear, tiger or elephant.
- Write an article about your animals then make a poster. Use the words in the boxes.

in forests   in the sea   in rivers and lakes   on the ice cap

smaller   hotter   drier   dirtier

6 Technology

1 Look, think and answer.
1. What's Stella talking about?
2. Who wants to learn about computers?
3. Who knows about computers?
4. Who's thinking about music?

- email
- screen
- the internet
- MP3 player
- DVD
- mouse
- button
- computer

2 🔊 CD2 21 Listen and check.

3 🔊 CD2 22 Listen and repeat. Say the letter.

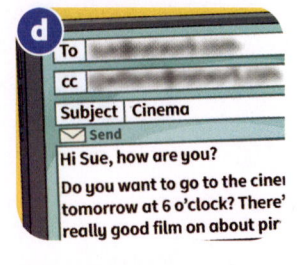

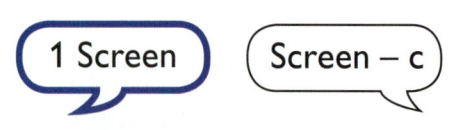

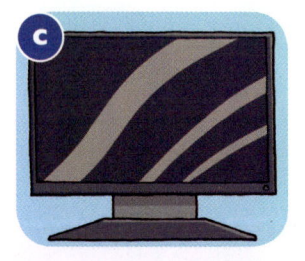

1 Screen — Screen – c

a, b, c, d, e, f

4 🎧 **Listen and match.** 1 – e

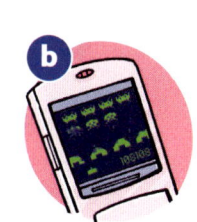

Grandpa needs a new mobile, (No, I don't!)
With an MP3. (A what?)
It's got music and ⁽¹⁾ video clips,
And lots, lots more to see. (I don't need any more!)

Grandpa needs a new mobile, (No, I don't!)
So he can ⁽²⁾ text his friends. (I can talk to my friends!)
He can take lots of ⁽³⁾ photos,
And play ⁽⁴⁾ games at weekends. (I go fishing at weekends!)

Grandpa! (I've got a DVD player at home!)
Grandpa! (I've got a nice camera!)
Grandpa! (And my old mobile phone works perfectly well!)
Grandpa needs a new mobile. (A new mobile phone!)

Grandpa needs a new mobile, (No, I don't!)
So he can ⁽⁵⁾ plan his day. (I've got a pen and paper!)
He can listen to lots of ⁽⁶⁾ songs,
And ⁽⁷⁾ phone or even play. (I haven't got time to play! I've got a radio!
I've got a nice camera! My old mobile phone works perfectly well! Hmph!)

5 🎧 **Sing the song.**

6 **Ask and answer. Use the words in the box.**

Has your grandpa got a mobile phone?   No, he hasn't.   Can you use a computer?   Yes, I can.

computer   TV   camera   the internet
mobile phone   email   e-book   video   app

7 Look, think and answer.
1 Where did Grandma and Grandpa go yesterday?
2 What did they get?
3 What's their computer called?
4 What problem have they got?

today

yesterday

LATEST models
BEST price

KBX4

8 🎧 26 CD2 Listen and check.

9 Complete the text.

| said   knew   put   ~~bought~~   thought   read   brought   chose |

Grandma and Grandpa went shopping yesterday. They **bought** a computer. They chose a KBX4 because Grandma _____ about it and the man in the shop _____ it was better than the others. The man _____ it home later. He took it out of the box, _____ it on the table and _____ goodbye. He thought they _____ the KBX4 because they _____ about computers!

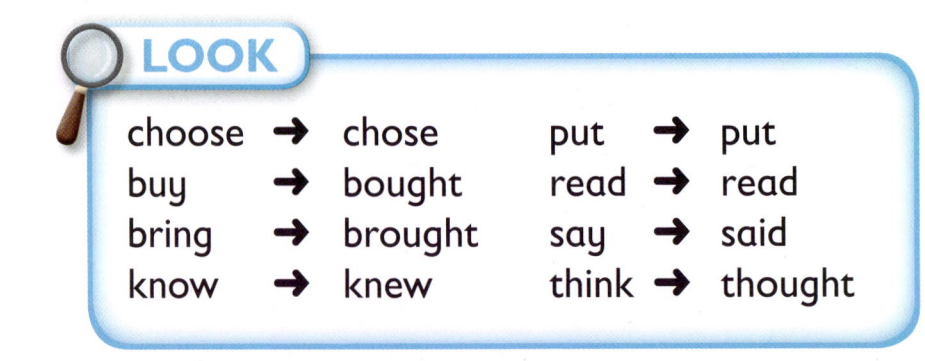

LOOK

choose	→	chose	put	→	put
buy	→	bought	read	→	read
bring	→	brought	say	→	said
know	→	knew	think	→	thought

10 🎧 **Listen and correct the actions.**

Jim's got a new computer game called Kid City. The people in his game do different things every day. Look at what they did yesterday.

> At 7 o'clock John got dressed.

> No. At 7 o'clock John got up.

yesterday

1. John
2. Mary
3. John
4. Jack
5. Peter / Sue
6. Jack
7. Mary
8. Mary
9. Sue
10. Peter
11. Mary
12. Peter

11 **Look at the pictures. Ask and answer.**

> What time did Mary get dressed?

> She got dressed at 8 o'clock.

12 **Write sentences about your day yesterday. Tell your friend.**

I got up at seven o'clock yesterday.

13 Stella's phonics

Paul caught a short fish.

His daughter bought a small ball.

The fish played with the ball in the water.

14 Make questions. Ask and find your partner.

What did you do yesterday morning?

I got up at eight o'clock …

What did you do yesterday morning?

I got up at seven o'clock …

30 CD2

LOCK & KEY

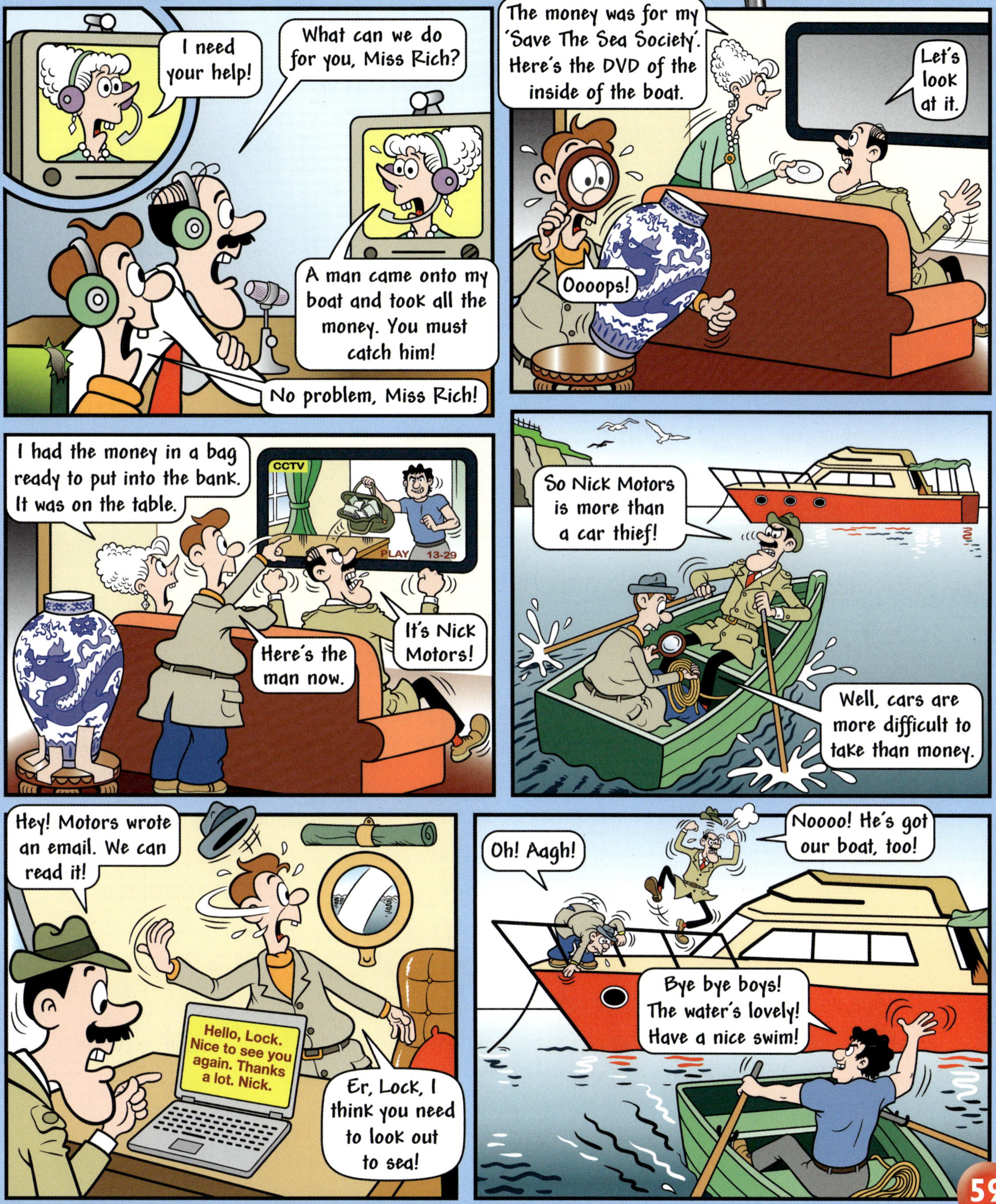

Technology — Robots

Fact: The first humanoid robot was designed by Leonardo da Vinci, in 1495.

1 Read and match.

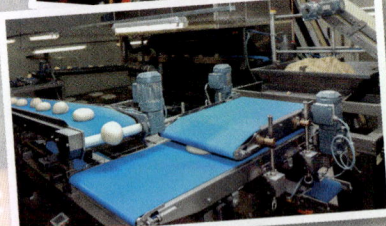

a.

b.

c.

1 At home we have a lot of machines. There are machines which clean the floor, wash and dry our clothes and wash the plates. In the kitchen there are machines which can make our breakfast, lunch and dinner. Some people call these machines kitchen robots, but what is a robot?

2 A robot is a machine which makes work easier for humans. They do jobs which humans can't do because they are very difficult or dangerous. Robots can explore places where humans can't go. They can go where there are dangerous gases or high temperatures: underground, underwater or in space.

3 Robots are very important because they make, build and fix things. It's easier for robots to work in factories because they can do the same job again and again and it isn't boring for them. Robots don't need money or holidays. They are never ill or tired, but they can't think. Robots can only do what humans program them to do.

2 🎧 31 CD2 Listen and say 'yes' or 'no'.

3 Read and match. Answer the questions.

a   b   c

Robots aren't the same as humans. They haven't got bodies like ours, but they have got three important parts.
1. They've got a computer program. This tells the robot what to do.
2. They've sometimes got legs which can make the robot move along the floor.
3. They've got sensors. The sensors help the robot to 'see' and to know where things are. The sensors are sometimes cameras.

1. How many important parts have robots got?
2. What tells the robot what to do?
3. What can make the robot move?
4. What helps the robot know where things are?
5. Where can the robot move?

Project Design a robot.

Review Units 5 and 6

1 Play the game. What did they do yesterday?

Instructions
1. Roll the dice and go around the board.
2. Say what each person did yesterday.
3. If your sentence is correct, stay where you are.
4. If your sentence is wrong, go back to where you were.

2 Read the story and complete the sentences.
Use 1, 2 or 3 words.

Shopping trip

Last Wednesday Alex went shopping with his mother, Pat. They went to town by bus and had a burger in a café before they went to the shops. Alex's mum wanted to buy a new bike for his younger sister, Jill. It was her birthday on Friday. The name of the toyshop was Pete's Toys. They bought Jill a new red bike and took it home on the bus.

1 Alex and ____his____ ____mother____ went shopping last Wednesday.
2 They ate _____ in a café.
3 Jill is Alex's _____.
4 They bought Jill _____.
5 On Friday it was _____ birthday.
6 Jill's bike was _____.
7 They went home _____.

Quiz!

1 How did Shackleton and his men lose their ship?
2 Who is more famous for his work, Cousteau or Shackleton?
3 Where did Nick Motors have dinner?
4 What do you hold in your hand when you use a computer?
5 Which computer did Grandma and Grandpa buy?
6 What did Nick Motors write?

7 At the zoo

1 Look, think and answer.
1. What are Lenny and Stella doing?
2. Who's asking the questions?
3. What's the quiz about?
4. Who do you think is winning?

Kid's Box Quiz Final

2 🎧 33 CD2 Listen and check.

3 🎧 34 CD2 Listen and say 'yes' or 'no'.

1 Lenny thinks the most exciting animal is the giraffe.

No.

LOOK

quick	→	the **quickest**
big	→	the **biggest**
exciting	→	the **most exciting**
beautiful	→	the **most beautiful**
good	→	the **best**

64

4 Read and correct.

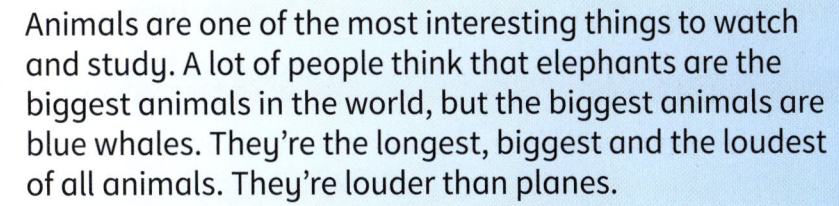

Fred's Blog

Animals are one of the most interesting things to watch and study. A lot of people think that elephants are the biggest animals in the world, but the biggest animals are blue whales. They're the longest, biggest and the loudest of all animals. They're louder than planes.

One of the smallest animals in the world is a lizard. It's between one and two centimetres long. The quickest animal is a bird which can fly at more than three hundred kilometres an hour.

The cleverest animals are humans, that's us! Some people think that monkeys are the second cleverest, but they aren't. Dolphins are cleverer than monkeys.

My favourite animals are tigers. I think they're the most exciting and most beautiful animals.

1 Kangaroos are the biggest animals.
2 Bears are the loudest animals.
3 One of the smallest animals in the world is a rabbit.
4 The quickest animals are lizards.
5 Monkeys are the second cleverest animals.
6 Fred thinks pandas are the most exciting animals.

5 What do you think? Write sentences.

beautiful   exciting   boring   clever   ugly   dangerous

I think the rabbit is the most boring animal here.

65

6 Look, think and answer.
1. Where did the children go?
2. Who did Suzy give her picture to?
3. What animals did they feed?
4. Which animal did Simon like the best?

drew   came   drove   saw   swam   slept   went
flew   bought   sat   caught   ate   ran   fed

7 Listen and check.

8 Listen and say the letter.

1 Mr Star drove the children to the zoo.

a

LOOK
What **did** he **buy**?
He **bought** a toy parrot.
He **didn't buy** an ice cream.

9 🎧 **Listen and do the actions.**

10 🎧 **Listen and sing.**

The elephants drank, drank, drank,
The parrots flew, flew, flew,
The dolphins swam, swam, swam,
At the zoo, zoo, zoo.

The elephants drank, drank, drank,
The parrots flew, flew, flew,
The dolphins swam, swam, swam,
At the zoo, zoo, zoo.

What did you do,
What did you do,
What did you do,
When you saw, saw, saw them
At the zoo, zoo, zoo?

The monkeys ate, ate, ate,
The children drew, drew, drew,
The lions slept, slept, slept,
At the zoo, zoo, zoo.

The monkeys ate, ate, ate,
The children drew, drew, drew,
The lions slept, slept, slept,
At the zoo, zoo, zoo.

What did you do,
What did you do,
What did you do,
When you saw, saw, saw them
At the zoo, zoo, zoo?

When you saw, saw, saw them
At the zoo, zoo, zoo?

11 **Write another verse for the song.**

The crocodiles smiled, smiled, smiled,
The giraffes ………, ………, ………,
The tigers ………, ………, ………,
At the zoo, zoo, zoo.

crocodile   giraffe
   tiger   panda
   snake   bat

smile   dance
jump   laugh
climb   hop

LOOK

out of     into    round    along

12 Stella's phonics

Sue's a kangaroo at the zoo.

She's looking in her cookbook.

Look! The animals at the zoo love Sue's blue juice!

13 Make questions. Ask and answer.

Which animal is the loudest?

I think elephants are the loudest.

snail   shark   panda   penguin   kangaroo   elephant

ugliest   slowest   most dangerous   quickest   loudest   smallest

Which animal is the … ?	name 1	name 2	name 3	name 4	name 5	name 6
loudest						
most dangerous						

LOCK & KEY

Nick Motors. Now you're the most wanted man in town.

Excuse me.

♪ RING!

Lock here.

Mr Lock, I'm phoning from the City Zoo. Please come quickly. We need your help.

Come on, Key. It's not the best time to play with Miss Rich's dog. We've got a job to do!

Ooops! Aagh! Ouch!

No problem, Lock. Er, goodbye, Miss Rich.

What's the problem, sir?

A man just took one of our lorries from outside the snake house.

Was this the man?

Yes! That's him! He rode into the zoo on that motorbike, and he drove out of it in our lorry!

My motorbike! My motorbike!

We can catch this thief and get the lorry for you.

Ha, ha, ha!

Hee, hee, hee!

Nice cat! Oooh, Mummy!

ROAR! SNARL!

Oh! The thief's got the biggest problem! There was a tiger inside the lorry!

Science — Skeletons

Fact: Instead of bones, sharks have a skeleton made from cartilage.

1 Look and read. Correct the sentences.

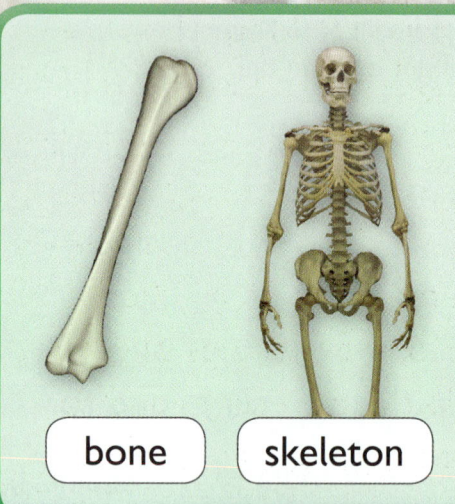

There are 206 bones in the human body. More than half of these are in the hands and feet. Bones are about 22 per cent water. The smallest bone in the body is in the ear and the longest bone is in the leg. Most bones have calcium in them. Human skeletons aren't very different from the skeletons of other animals. A human has got the same number of neck bones as a giraffe!

bone   skeleton

1. There are two hundred bones in the human body.
2. All our bones are in our hands and feet.
3. The smallest bone in our body is in the arm.
4. The shortest bone is in the leg.
5. A human has got the same number of feet bones as a giraffe.

2 Look at the four skeletons. Which animals are they from?

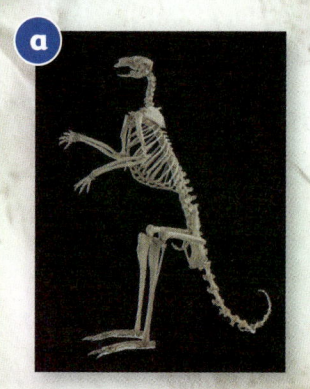

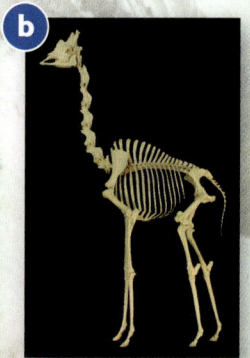

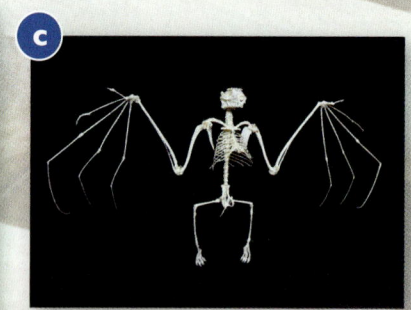

a   b   c   d

3 Read and match the animals to the skeletons.
1. This animal's got very long, strong wings to help it fly quickly.
2. This animal's got long arms and legs to climb trees in the jungle.
3. This animal's got a very long tail to help it stand up.
4. This animal's got very long neck bones to eat leaves from high trees.

4 Read and complete.

> giraffes   tail   Monkeys   long   Crocodiles   skeletons

Different animals have got different _____. This is because they live in different habitats and they have to do different things to live. Some animals fly, some swim, some run, some jump and some climb. _____ have got long, strong _____ bones. These help them to move quickly when they catch animals to eat. They've also got big eyes on the top of their heads. These stay out of the water looking for food when the rest of its body is under water. The leaves which _____ eat are at the top of high trees, so they need very _____ neck bones to get them. _____ have often got long arms, legs and tails. These help them to climb and to move more quickly from tree to tree. They sometimes need to run away from other bigger, hungrier animals!

5 Listen and say 'yes' or 'no'.

Project

Make a class comic of 'Super Animals'.

- Think of two or three different animals and their skeletons.
- What can they do with their different bones and body parts?
- What's your Super Animal called?
- What body parts has it got?
- What can it do?

8 Let's party!

1 Look, think and answer.
1 Whose birthday is it today?
2 What are the grown-ups doing?
3 What kind of sandwiches are there?
4 Who's thirsty?

- bottle
- box
- bowl
- vegetables
- cup
- cheese
- sandwich
- soup
- salad
- pasta
- glass

2 Listen and check.

3 Listen and say the letter.

1 A bowl of salad. — a

a b  c d
e  f  g h

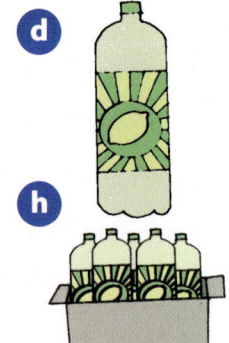

4 🔊 **Listen and say the letter.**

1 Can you take these dirty cups to the kitchen please, children? → b

a He wants her to make a cheese sandwich.

b She wants them to take the cups to the kitchen.

c He wants him to pass the bowl of salad.

d She wants him to hold the glass.

e They want her to open the bottle of lemonade.

f He wants them to put the glasses on the table.

5 **Read and correct.**

Paul wants to make lunch for his mum and dad. He wants his brother and sister to help him. He wants Vicky to make a bowl of salad and then he wants her to make a bowl of soup. He wants Jack to take a plate of sandwiches and a bottle of lemonade to the table. After lunch he wants him to make a cup of coffee for their parents. Paul wants to sit down and watch TV with a glass of apple juice. His brother and sister aren't happy, they're angry. They want Paul to help them.

1 Paul wants his mum and dad to help him.
2 He wants Vicky to make a box of noodles.
3 He wants her to make a cup of soup.
4 Paul wants Jack to take a plate of pancakes to the table.
5 He wants him to make a cup of coffee for their aunt and uncle.

6 Look, think and answer.
1. What are the children doing?
2. Who's first?
3. Who's last?
4. Who's walking?

7 🔊 Listen and check.

8 🔊 Listen and say the name.

1 He's jumping the most quickly.

Alex.

LOOK

quickly	→	the **most quickly**
slowly	→	the **most slowly**
well	→	the **best**
badly	→	the **worst**

9 Look at the pictures. Find the differences.

> In picture B the clown's drinking a milkshake.

10 Complete the song. Listen and check.

> made   ate   wore   ~~said~~   drank   danced   gave   was

We had soup, we had pasta,
We had salads and cheese.
We all wanted more,
We all _said_ 'please'.
We _____ presents,
And cards which we _____ .
We _____ fancy dress,
We _____ and we played …

The party was good,
The party _____ great.
And now it's time to fly.
The party was good,
The party was great.

We'll see you soon, goodbye.

The drinks we _____ ,
The food we _____ .
The party was good,
The party was great.

We gave presents …

Now the party's over,
Now it's time to fly.
See you soon, goodbye.

11 Sing the song.

75

12 Stella's phonics

Say **soup** and **blue**,
And **think**, **thought** and **flew**.
Say **wa**ter, **pas**ta and **cle**ver,
And **par**ty, **bot**tle and **wea**ther.
Another syllable will make it three,
Say **beau**tiful, **el**ephant and **care**fully!

13 Choose a picture. Play the game.

What am I?

Have you got a red nose?

No, I haven't.

Can you sail a boat?

Yes, I can.

LOCK & KEY

Let's go, Key! We have to work more carefully this time. We can't make any more mistakes.

Eeek! No problem, Lock!

ZOO

VROOOM!

Here, nice cat! Have a bag of parrot food! Mmmm!

Here's a bottle of water...

No? How about a nice box of ... fruit!

ROAR! ROAR!

Look, there it is! The lorry's over there!

Oh, yes. Now we've got him!

City ZOO

We've got you now, Nick. The police are coming to get you!

Oh, yes please. Take me away from the tiger. Thank you! You're my heroes!

Nice work, men. You caught Nick Motors for us!

Well, we had a little help.

No problem!

City ZOO

77

Science — Food

> **Fact**
> A 60 gram bar of milk chocolate has seven teaspoons of sugar in it.

1 Look at the food plate.
How often do you think you need to eat food from each group?

- Fruit and vegetables
- Carbohydrates
- Protein
- Fats and sugar
- Dairy products

2 Read and answer.

For a healthy body we need to eat different kinds of food. There are five important groups of food: carbohydrates; dairy products; fats and sugar; protein; fruit and vegetables.

Carbohydrates give us energy. (1) What kinds of food are carbohydrates?

Dairy products make our bones and teeth strong because they contain calcium. We get calcium from milk and food which comes from milk, like yoghurt. (2) Do you know another food which comes from milk?

Fats and sugar also give us energy, but a lot of fat and sugar is not good for our bodies. (3) What kinds of food have sugar? (4) What kinds of food have got fat?

Protein is important because it is good for our muscles and it makes them strong. Protein comes from animals or some vegetables, like beans. (5) What other foods do you think give us protein?

Fruit and vegetables have a lot of vitamins and minerals. (6) Can you say the names of five different fruits? (7) Can you name three different vegetables?

3 Read and match.   1 – e

Pasta salad

You need:
1. 2 tomatoes
2. 250 g pasta
3. 100 g cheese
4. 200 g chicken
5. 2 carrots
6. some lemon juice and oil

4 Read and order the sentences.   1 – f

Preparation:

a. Then cut the cheese into pieces and mix it in a big bowl with the tomatoes and carrots.
b. Now you can eat your pasta salad.
c. Next, cut the tomatoes and carrots into small pieces.
d. Second, cook the chicken. When it's cold, cut it into small pieces.
e. Last, put some oil and lemon juice over the salad.
f. First, cook the pasta in a lot of water.
g. Put the pasta and chicken into the bowl with the tomato, carrots and cheese.

Project   Write a recipe for your favourite lunch.

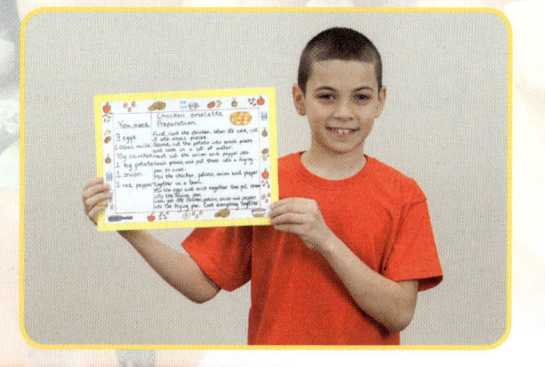

Review Units 7 and 8

1 Play the game.

Instructions

1. Groups of three or four.
2. Move and answer the questions. You only have 30 seconds.
- Right answer: stay.
- Wrong answer: go back one space.

START

1. Which animal lives in Antarctica?
2. Name five animals you can see at the zoo.
3. What's the fifteenth letter of the alphabet?
4. Say five 'clothes' words.
5. What's the opposite of 'dirtiest'?
6. Say five 'food' words.
7. How much is fifty-eight plus thirteen?
8. What's the past of 'think'?
9. What's the opposite of 'into'?
10. Say five 'job' words.
11. What's the past of 'choose'?
12. Say five 'school' words.
13. Which is the tallest animal?
14. What kind of animals can fly?
15. What's the past of 'know'?
16. Say five 'transport' words.
17. How much is forty-three and eighteen?
18. What's the opposite of 'outside'?
19. What's the past of 'drive'?
20. Say five 'technology' words.

FINISH!

2 Tell the story.

> Peter got up. He was sad. He wanted to play football outside, but the weather was terrible …

3 Now write the story.

Peter got up. He was sad. He wanted to play football outside, but the weather was terrible …

Quiz!
1 Who was in the Kid's Box Quiz Final?
2 What did the parrots do at the zoo?
3 What did Nick Motors take from the zoo?
4 What was there to eat at Simon's party?
5 Who jumped the most slowly in the sack race?
6 What did Nick Motors find inside the lorry?

Units 1 & 2 — Values — Value others

1 Look and think. Say 'yes' or 'no'.
1 When our friends help us at school, we say 'sorry'.
2 We can give flowers to people when we want to say thank you.
3 We say thank you to people when they help us.
4 When our parents give us a party, we say 'goodbye'.

2 Listen and check. (16 CD3)

3 Read and complete in pairs.

> our teacher.   them a letter.   and smile at them.
> they help us.   say thank you.   give them a picture.

"We say thank you to people when …"   "they help us."

1 We say thank you to people when …
2 We can give someone a present to …
3 When people help us, we can say thank you …
4 When we enjoy a school lesson we can say thank you to …
5 When we want to say thank you to people, we can …
6 To say thank you to someone we can sometimes write …

Be kind | **Values** | **Units 3 & 4**

1 Look and think. Say 'yes' or 'no'.
1. We can give our seat to older people on the bus.
2. It's good to help younger children with a problem.
3. We can ask old people to carry our bags.
4. We can stay on the toys in the park when other children are waiting to use them.

2 🔊 Listen and check.

3 Read and match.
1. If we see old people on a bus or train, we can …
2. If we see small children with problems, we can …
3. If we see an older person with a shopping bag, we can …
4. When other children want the same thing as us, …

a carry it for them.
b we can take turns.
c try to help them.
d stand up and give them our seat.

Units 5 & 6 Values — Be safe

1 Look and think. Say 'yes' or 'no'.
1. You can play near busy roads.
2. You can cross the road between cars.
3. You must stop, look and listen before you cross the road.
4. You must wear a helmet when you ride a bike.

2 Listen and check.

3 Read and complete in pairs.

> use it to cross the road.   can't see you.   busy roads.
> ~~ride a bike.~~   before you cross the road.

Remember to put on a helmet when you … — ride a bike.

1. Remember to put on a helmet when you …
2. Don't stand between cars when you cross the road. Drivers …
3. Don't play next to …
4. Remember to stop, look and listen …
5. When there is a zebra crossing always …

Recycle **Values** **Units 7 & 8**

1 Look and think. Say 'yes' or 'no'.
 1 We must put plastic and paper into special bins.
 2 We mustn't recycle glass.
 3 We can make things from old clothes.
 4 We mustn't recycle clothes.

2 🔊 Listen and check.

3 Read and match.
 1 When we can't reuse things, we …
 2 Make plastic bottles smaller …
 3 Always put paper, glass, plastic and cans …
 4 We can make new things …

 a from old clothes.
 b into the right recycling bins.
 c before you recycle them.
 d can sometimes recycle them.

85

Grammar reference

Grandpa Star's older than Mr Star.
The dog's bigger than the cat.
Uncle Fred's funnier than Aunt May.

He sometimes has to get up at 5 o'clock.
She always has to work at the weekend.
He never has to do his homework on Saturday.

1

He's / She's the teacher who's wearing a red sweater.
They're the girls who are skipping.

2

What can I learn to do?	You can learn to sing.
What do you / they want to learn to do?	I / We / They want to learn to paint. I / We / They don't want to learn to roller skate.
What does he / she want to learn to do?	He / She wants to learn to dance. He / She doesn't want to learn to ride a horse.
What's the Activity Centre?	It's a place where you can learn to swim.

3

I / You / He / She / It / We / They	had / didn't have lunch at school.
Did you see the dentist last year? Did he / she eat chocolate cake?	Yes, I did. / No, I didn't. Yes, he / she did. / No, he / she didn't.
How many ice creams did you have?	I had two ice creams. / I didn't have an ice cream.

Her mum gave her medicine I had a drink They ate a sandwich	because	she had a headache. I was hot. they were hungry.

4

What did Alex need? Where did she live? Who did Mr Burke stop? What did Simon carry?	Alex needed a hat and a scarf. She lived in a big town. Mr Burke stopped Simon. Simon carried the boxes.

5

They were hungry		they ate an apple.
It was cold	so	they had a hot drink.
I couldn't find my map		I got lost.

interesting → more interesting	This film is more interesting than that one.
famous → more famous	She is more famous than him.
difficult → more difficult	Maths homework is more difficult than English homework.

My bike goes more slowly than yours.
He rides his bike more carefully than her.

6

What did you buy?	I bought / didn't buy a new MP3 player.
Where did he put the DVD?	He put / didn't put it on the table.
What did they think?	They thought / didn't think the internet was slow.
What did she know?	She knew / didn't know the song on the radio.

7

quick → quicker → the quickest	It's the quickest lizard in the world.
beautiful → more beautiful → the most beautiful	Blue whales are the most beautiful animals.
good → better → the best	I think rabbits are the best pets.

What did you eat?	I ate / didn't eat the cake.
What did he / she see?	He / She saw / didn't see a dolphin.
Where did they / we swim?	They / We swam / didn't swim in the sea.

8

| slowly → more slowly → the most slowly | The woman's walking the most slowly. |
| carefully → more carefully → the most carefully | The boys are riding the most carefully. |

blank page

Movers practice test — Listening

Part **1** 5 questions

Listen and draw lines. There is one example.

Vicky   Peter   Mary   Paul

Daisy   Jim   Fred

Part 2　5 questions

Listen and write. There is one example.

The village

	When?	Friday
1	Talked to	
2	Biggest animals	
3	Animals' food	
4	Name of village	
5	Number of people in village	

Part 3 5 questions

What sport does Peter do in these places?
Listen and write a letter in each box. There is one example.

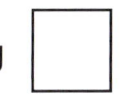

running — H	fishing — ☐
climbing — ☐	swimming — ☐
riding a bike — ☐	horse riding — ☐

A B  C  D  E  F  G  H

Part 4   5 questions

Listen and tick (✓) the box. There is one example.

What was the weather like last weekend?

1 Where did Alex go after school?

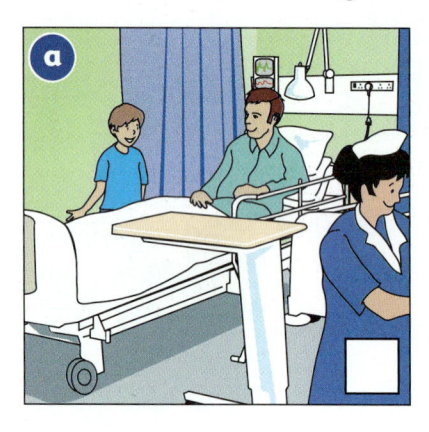

2 What did they do at the party?

3 What did the man buy?

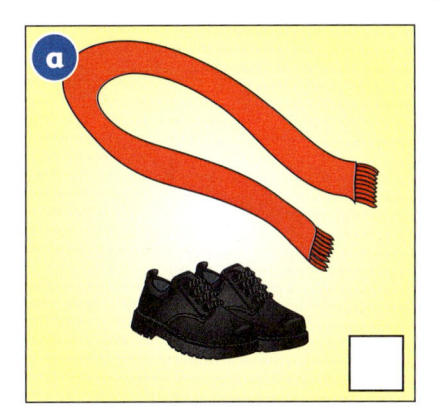

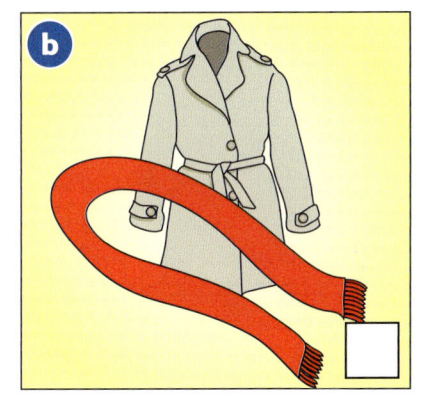

a   b   c

4 Where do the aliens live?

a   b   c

5 Which zoo animals did the girl like?

a   b   c

Part 5 5 questions

Listen and colour and write. There is one example.

Movers practice test — Reading & Writing

Part 1 5 questions

Look and read. Choose the correct words and write them on the lines. There is one example.

a neck    penguins    kittens 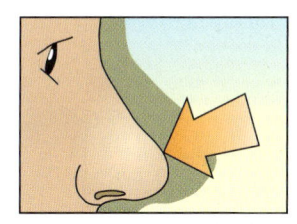   a nose

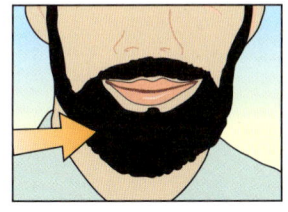

a beard    rabbits    mice 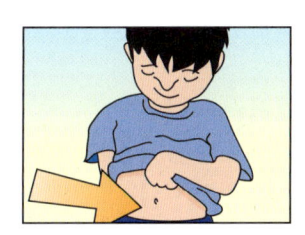   a stomach

Example

These pet animals are baby cats.   kittens

Questions

1 When you eat, your food and drink goes here.   _____
2 These animals can swim.   _____
3 This is between your head and your shoulders.   _____
4 This is on your face, between your eyes and your mouth.   _____
5 These animals have big ears. They eat grass.   _____

Part 2   6 questions

Read the text and choose the best answer.

Example

Miss Grey: Hello, Jack. Why are you sitting there?
Jack: **A** I can't walk home.
    B It doesn't work.
    C I'm not walking.

Questions

1 **Miss Grey:** Oh dear! What's the matter?
  Jack: A It doesn't matter.
       B I hurt my foot.
       C It hurt me.

2 **Miss Grey:** When did you do that?
  Jack: A After school this afternoon.
       B I didn't do it.
       C I'm sorry.

3 Miss Grey: Don't cry! I can help you. Where do you live?
Jack: **A** It's a big house.
       B At home.
       C In Bath Street.

4 Miss Grey: Is there a bus to your house?
Jack: **A** No, I haven't got a ticket.
       B No, we always walk.
       C No, but I like going by bus.

5 Miss Grey: Have you got your phone with you?
Jack: **A** No. He hasn't got one.
       B No. I lost it yesterday.
       C No. There isn't a phone.

6 Miss Grey: Well, do you want to phone your mum?
Jack: **A** Yes, please!
       B Yes, you do.
       C Yes, it would.

Part 3 6 questions

Read the story. Choose a word from the box.
Write the correct word next to numbers 1–5.
There is one example.

The Flying Shark was a very famous pirate ship. Everyone was afraid of the pirates from this ship. But one day they got lost. They ____sailed____ to an island to look for treasure. They looked and looked but they couldn't find any because there was a mistake on their **(1)** _____ . They were on the wrong island! The pirates were very **(2)** _____.
In the morning it was very hot but there was nothing to eat or drink. Now they didn't want treasure. They wanted food and **(3)** _____.
Then they heard someone calling to them from the trees. It said, 'Coconuts and bananas. Coconuts and bananas.' The pirates ran to see who it was. But it wasn't a person, it was some **(4)** _____. There were lots of coconuts and bananas in the trees. They **(5)** _____ the bananas and drank milk from the coconuts.
'This is better than treasure,' they said.

Example

sailed

beach

water

map

read

angry

happy

parrots

ate

(6) Now choose the best name for the story.
Tick one box.

The beautiful treasure ☐

The terrible weather ☐

The hungry pirates ☐

Part 4   5 questions

Read the text. Choose the right words and write them on the lines.

Sharks

Example — Sharks are fish. They ____don't____ like cold water.

1 They live in the sea in hot parts _____ the world.

They catch smaller fish and sea animals, which they

2 _____ with their strong teeth.

Some people say that sharks never fall asleep, but this is

3 wrong. They sleep, but _____ eyes are always

4 open and they never stop _____ .

There are many different kinds of sharks. The biggest

5 ones are white. People _____ afraid of them,

but most sharks are small and they can't hurt you.

Example	doesn't	don't	didn't
1	on	at	of
2	ate	eat	eaten
3	her	its	their
4	moving	moves	move
5	is	are	be

Part 5   7 questions

Look at the pictures and read the story.
Write some words to complete the sentences about the story. You can use 1, 2 or 3 words.

A nice Saturday

'What can I do?' Jane asked her mum on Saturday morning. 'Let's go to the supermarket!' Mum said. 'We can do the shopping and then make lunch.' 'I hate shopping,' Jane said. 'It's boring.'

'OK,' Mum said, 'I've got a better idea.' She phoned Jane's grandma. 'Bring Jane to me,' Grandma said. 'I love having her here.'

They got in the car and drove to Grandma's flat. Grandma opened the door and said, 'Come on, Jane, we must go shopping. Let's buy some nice food.'

Examples

Mum wanted to go to the supermarket on ___Saturday morning___.

Jane didn't want to go ___shopping___ with her mum.

Questions

1 Mum had a good _____ and she phoned Jane's grandma.

2 Mum took Jane to Grandma's flat by _____ .

Grandma took Jane to a market in the street near her flat. They bought lots of good things – vegetables, pasta, bread and a bottle of juice. Jane carried it all in a big bag. She took it upstairs carefully.

3 Jane and Grandma bought lots of nice things to eat at _____.

4 They put all the food in _____ and carried it to Grandma's flat.

Grandma cooked the pasta. Jane made a salad. 'It's sunny today,' Grandma said. 'Let's eat on the balcony.' They sat and enjoyed their lunch. 'I like your salad, Jane,' Grandma said. 'It's very good.' Then Mum phoned. 'I'm having a great day,' Jane told her. 'We went shopping and made lunch.' Mum laughed. 'Oh, Jane, you are funny!' she said.

5 Jane and Grandma had lunch on _____.

6 The _____ which Jane made was very good.

7 Mum thought it was _____ when Jane said, 'I'm having a great day'.

Part 6 6 questions

Look and read and write.

Examples

The woman has got <u>curly black</u> hair.
What is the small girl playing with? <u>two toy cars</u>

Complete the sentences.

1 The man _____ football with a boy.
2 The woman and the girl are sitting _____ .

Answer the questions.

3 Where is the cat? _____
4 What are the girl and boy with blond hair wearing on their feet?
_____

Now write two sentences about the picture.

5 _____
6 _____